Murder Bear

Murder Bear

W. N. Herbert

Donut Press

Published by Donut Press in 2013

Donut Press,
The Cobwebs,
12 West Street,
Ashburton,
Devon,
TQ13 7DU.
www.donutpress.co.uk

ISBN: 9780956644572

Contents

...I remember
I am not here, only the space
I sent the terrible beast across.
Watch. He bites.

W.S. Graham, 'The Beast in the Space'

The Four Bears

Of course Daddy Bear never mentioned
his missing brother, Murder, nor that
he wasn't missing at all, but in the loft
the whole time Baby Bear was downstairs
in the bed beside Mummy's and Daddy's,
dreaming about a girl who once lay between
his sheets, who perfumes his pillow still
with her grassy fresh air sweat. Had we all
been aware that it was Murder Bear
who fell down the ladder like a shadow,
crossing out the sunlight cast through
the curtain in the shower, and took off
a cloud of her golden hair with one claw
and most of her face with the other,
we should not have been so anxious
to lock Baby Bear's mother and father up
in Polar Penitentiary. How Daddy Bear
persuaded the others not to squeal
we do not know. Only that after the trial
Baby returned to the disembowelled house
(his uncle having fled into the forest
to dwell among the gory leavings of autumn),
there to sleep in the same bed, eat
at the same table, and contemplate
the temperature of the blood that pours
through his veins. It's Baby Bear temperature.
Upon the plain scrubbed table before him
remains her bowl, filled with golden hair.

A Night Story

Once upon a time there was a Murder Bear.
Then he killed everyone. The End.

…

Why aren't you asleep yet?
'You frightened me talking about Murder Bear.'

Well, you don't need to be afraid of Murder Bear unless he finds you.
'He isn't going to find me, is he?'

Yes. Yes he is going to find you:
Murder Bear finds everyone eventually.

'How can he tell?'
By your sweet, sweet smell.

'Does he kill everyone?'
D'uh. The clue is in the name.

'Does he kill Goldilocks?'
'Goldilocks is no longer with us.'

'Does he kill Paddington?'
Yes, he really goes to town on Paddington.

'Does he kill Postman Pat?'
He beats him to death with his own cat.

'Does he kill Blue Peter?'
With a parking meter.

'Does he kill News at Ten?'
With a fountain pen.

'Does he kill the X Factor?'
He takes the judges out with a tractor.

'Does he kill Harry Potter?'
There is a considerable amount of J.K. Rowling-related slaughter.

'When is he coming for me?'
Once he's dealt with your poor parental units.

'You can beat him, though, can't you?'
I thought I'd explained there really is no hope. Now go to sleep.

…

'Night night.'
Night, Honey Bun.

Murder Bear and the Makie-up People

Murder Bear kept his honey in a row
of skulls along the mantelpiece although
these were the noggins of fictional detectives.
But as he'd neither fire nor place to rest
his wiry head, that hardly seemed to matter.
Mater Ursa used to leave him notes concerning
the whereabouts of bootprints of the novelists:
'By the trail of paper entrails ye shall know them…'
'…and by the ten thousand flapping ghosts
of golden luckless lasses I shall hunt them down,
for Jesus saith…' he'd reply, not at all averse
to the removal of scripture from its abdomen
by keyhole claw, 'that "Whosoever looketh on
the genre of horribly-tortured women
hath committed Murder Bear unto his heart."'
'And anyway…' – bursting through the chalet walls
in a conversational tone, walls that once had looked
so stout of timber and now were found to be
a forgery in Toblerone and matchwood –
'you have to excorticate to desanguinate,
or, othergates, butcher the scribblers before
they can kill off their darkling constables
and other dicks…'; ripping out their sinful hearts
and shameful tongues, and bearing back
their thumbs and delicious typing appendages
to roast upon his flameless forest grate.

A Murderous Sestina

'You don't really come here for the hunting, do you?' (A punchline)

Murder Bear knows nothing of humour, only the thunder
between his temples that announces another apartment
must be varnished in blood before the flit up-country
to where mist makes the mountains frown. But pleasant
ribaldry dictates that in these woods, buttocks scratched
with Twig Sumerian, teeth flecked with spinach,

a hunter must cower behind – what is this, spinach?
How would he know? – while the roar like thunder
of a grizzly, enraged at his bullet that has scratched
her shoulder, reverberates within the log apartment
he'd rented for the weekend, thinking it would be pleasant
to reconnect with someone's roots, far from Rutabaga County.

Which is why Murder Bear briefly considers country
matters, given the joke's logic and the quantities of spinach
he's eaten en route, lending a not-unpleasant
vigour to his step and other appetites; but thunder
announces our autumnal rains, so to the apartment
he repairs, its furniture much chewed and scratched

by the grizzly, a dearest coz whose head he'd scritched
when she was GRARGH-high, back in that other country
before the first neck-snappings. They tidy the apartment
and have dinner, venison steaks and further spinach;
while the hunter times his howls to match the thunder,
they spend a firelit hour in complicit pleasantries,

as though Cape Fear could ever be Mount Pleasant,
but soon blind rage returns, the way that lightning has scratched
out the hunter's eyes – a need inevitable as thunder
drives MB, twitch-clawed, out into night's country
to shred his victim's skin as though a chard or spinach,
then burn him shrieking in his well-insured apartment.

Next morning, kicking through the spars of the apartment,
he finds the hunter's trousers, folded and complacent
upon a blackened chair, remembers the spinach
between those knocked-out teeth, and sees he's barely scratched
the surface of his cousin or this fucked-up country,
feeling as stupid as the lisping God of Thunder,

Thor. There's still tinned spinach in the apartment;
she's gone like lightning but, thunderously humming pleasant
airs, he follows her message north, scratched across his country.

from Murder Bear's Address to the Polar Explorers

…I see you're not as fascinated by the way
the page makes so strange a mirror
to our imagined meanings as am I.
Your eyes are far more drawn to this
ice-axe: perhaps you wonder how,
thumb-less, I grip it so very tightly.
And yet you came here to ask
a similar question of all this snow:

'What can we mean where we do not matter?'
and not, 'Who is the bear that stalks beside you?'

If you were indeed taught writing by a bird
(Thoth, that long-legged god of the papyrus),
then warned against it by a wise Athenian
(Socrates, fearing the murder of memory),
next, advised *contre interpretation* by
of all nationalities a Frenchman
(my dear Montaigne, who schools you not
to 'fill posterity with crotchets'),

then where shall paradox end but on the edge
of this, your finely-honed ice-axe?

To reverse language's polarity, it is
the space in the beast which concerns you
here – that which does not come across
to you, cranial astronauts, who cannot know
how I do not think I am and therefore must
travel to your inner stars' menageries,
dig to your circus of the lower rings: limbic,
reptile, then the notochordate worm.

See how the ice-axe gleams in the brevity
of the sun: think of it as Hackem's Razor.

I shall address you and these questions to
the crevasse, since it never asks
and cannot answer the blue telephone
far below, like a meaning in an ink-stroke
pressed into this page of flattened stars
like an anti-mountain, mould for Mont Blanc –
please pick up if it should ring
while you are passing.

The Passionate Psychobear To His Love

Come dine with me and share this rug
and shrive our guilt with half a shrug:
the lovers who dined here before
won't need their picnic anymore.

They've set aside first fork and glass
then mortal things – all this must pass –
and should their heads prove hard to find,
their fingers still lie here entwined.

That salmon slapping on your plate:
bite off its tail, it shan't escape.
Then with my littlest claw…now, lo!
observe its pomegranate roe.

Each rosy orb that parts your lips
shall add unto the blood eclipse
I'll visit on the fauna which
disturb our realm with fence and ditch.

Each logger, jogger, fisher, witch
shall find their hike has met its hitch:
I'll raise you a mountain from their arms,
though off they run with shrill alarums.

This wilderness shall be your park:
no nightingale disturbs your dark –
the shriek-owl's song's more to our taste.
All this for you I shall lay waste.

All seasons must bow down before
your gelid eye, or drown in gore:
this bucket for your throne of ice,
gaze on our ursine paradise.

Bear Grills Bear Grylls

Survivalist-journos rarely outlived a day
   in the company of Murder Bear –
ephemerons and mumble-newses to his purview,
   they learnt to rue that urge to interview
which drove them to his hills, rich in pineals,
   where he'd scoop their quaking innards
onto the barbecue. Hanging with him was not
   drawn-out in such close quarters
where he'd query, 'Learn to share: what was it
   in your upbringing led you to suppose
everyone could be reduced to a mere mots jus?'
   Woodsmen didn't take to his tendency
to reuse their signature sinews and living ligaments
   as catapults, sending evidences of
our frail humanities through the forest canopies
   to be picked over by editor jays,
scat-speckled squirrels and bespectacled pies.
   Smears of Ray Mears still appear,
contaminating crime labs and delis across
   three states. Though Butcher Bird
and Carrion Crow study the DVD evidence
   of his interrogation technique,
all he'll say of The Death of a Thousand Offcuts is
   'The victim needs no expertise.'

Hendecakillabics for the Restive Season

In the month of the marked increase in shopping,
by his donning a slightly-chewed-up man-suit
(victim chosen for having such a fat head,
though it's still quite a squeeze to cram his ears in),
the most murderous of bears will pass among us
on the metro, the bus, the escalator,
in the cafes and bars that warm large cities,
and select his exciting Christmas victim.
While old humbugs may sit unscathed beside him,
the unduly punctilious buyers of slippers
and insisters on proper thankyou letters
may expect an unusual midnight visit
and their neatly-wrapped skin ripped open roughly
till their seasonal lights festoon the fir tree.
'Tis the time of the year to clean his rifle
as he hopes that old fool presents a target
he can aim at upon the yuletide rooftops,
then it's out with the hunting knife for Rudolf.
In the meantime there's always office parties
to be crashed and then photocopied bleeding
from each orifice; boss and secretary
bound together and flung into the river
in a touching noyade of class relations.
Always drunks to be nudged off station platforms,
little match girls to sauté by flame-thrower,
snowmen needing to eat their magic top hats,
anxious mothers who must see all their trimmings,
lazy fathers who need a shot of buckshot.
It's a miracle how he gets around us

all in just one night, but a bear must do in
whom a bear (so the voices claim) must do in.
So you be just as good, or bad, or ugly
as your conscience sees fit, because the main thing's
to be lucky and quick and unobtrusive
like a rat or a strain of flu or music
that might soothe this most savage beast: no carols,
please, unless you can live without your larynx,
though a phrase from the Stranglers or old Sweeney
(if your whistle be wet) might mean he walks on
by, the wing of Death's angel fails to beat in
your face, eyes screwed shut, heart, for now, still beating;
heart still serving up blood in pints. Go, bootsteps;
heart, relax; and those nails, release the brickwork –
then his whisper: '*I hear you when you're weeping…*'

Didst Thou Ever See Murder Bear?

(A Shandean Digression & Found Poem)

MURDER BEAR! Very well.
Have I ever seen him?
Might I ever have seen him?
Am I ever to see him?
Ought I ever to see him?
Or can I ever see him?

Would I had seen Murder Bear!
(for how can I imagine it?)
If I should see Murder Bear,
what should I say?
If I should never see Murder Bear,
what then?

If I never have, can, must or shall
see Murder Bear alive;
have I ever seen him dead?
If so, which of us was thus?
Did I ever see him painted? – described?
Have I ever dreamed of him?

Did my father, mother, brothers or sisters,
ever see Murder Bear?
What would they give?
How would they behave?
How would Murder Bear have behaved?
Is he wild? Tame? Terrible? Rough? Smooth?

– Is Murder Bear worth seeing? –
– Is there no sin in him? –
– Is he better than a TEDDY BEAR?

Murder Bear Has the Last Words

Murder Bear was an endgame hunter and, indeed,
as the Amazon river dolphin found out, fisher.
Once he'd played midnight's chimes to the Sun bear
and was Cassandra to the ultimate Panda;

once he'd been an Ahab to the Gobi bear
('How a harpoon in the desert amazes the Mazaalai!')
and had made a spectacle of *Tremarctos ornatus*
('A giant burning lens focuses both mind and eye!),

he turned to the terminal languages, sitting
with their grey-faced speakers for hours, grizzling
along, mastering the lilt if not the meaning,
as they told their fables for the final time.

When he heard the two last speakers of Ayapeneco
refused to talk to each other, he determined
to referee between them, as to who should truly
have the last word, which only he would hear.

Some tongues he collected like stamps –
Gaelic and Aramaic fascinated:
their dialects of Cain and Judas spoke to him;
he mouthed the phrasebooks of murder and betrayal.

He dealt with the alphabets alphabetically,
murmuring, 'Ainu, Bo, Cayuga, Dumi,
Evenki, Faroese, Guajiro…'. With the ideographs
he hit upon the graphic art of kill-igraphy.

He heard them plead their hopeless cases,
then laid out their dead declensions, mourning
as their dictionaries burned, 'I like a corpse
in cuneiform'; and keening, 'Ate in Akkadia, *Urso*.'

He sought, in those broken-off last words,
a different eloquence, and set about him
to reduce the world to its original dumbness,
a garden filled with that silence before sin

could be spoken of…

Murdered Sonnet

A reification a taxonomy and a teleology
walked into the bar where Murder Bear was in mid-
Stagger mode with a handgun and a hopelessness –
murderer of childhood's dream that every fate
is random but for yours, each death inevitable
except I shall be spared; killer of the ease
with which we believe that narrative applies
to our dreams and not to how we remember them;

despoiler of the garden where the wrinkles are
just tiredness, the hair loss only stress, and, look!
picker-offer of the dead as they return to us
over the river and under the trees, just as
they always said they would in the movie
where the hero is being eaten by his friend the bear.

Montaigne and the Three Murder Bears

Rain-allowing Graskolnikov, grim Moosebuggery,
who is the third whom the weather detains,
compelled to kill because we are too merry,
awaiting the approach of Monsieur de Montaigne?

Who is this third whom the weather detains,
who fidgets through packages under the trees,
awaiting the approach of Monsieur de Montaigne?
Perhaps he is counting his murderer's fee?

Who fidgets through packages under the trees
is often too nervous when in at the kill.
Perhaps he is doubting this murderous spree?
But no, he's located a box full of pills.

Those who get nervous when in at the kill
take physic from sack, read fortune from signs,
or else take their courage from boxes of pills –
but no, he has drawn and is first in the line.

Take physic from sack and read fortune from signs,
your death is upon you, Monsieur de Montaigne!
But no, though he's drawn and is first in the line,
he's gifting him pills and not giving him pains…

'When death is upon you, Monsieur de Montaigne,'
he whispers, while sweeping his cutlass at us,
'these pills for the quinsy and these for the pain.'
And now he has drawn a strange arquebus,

and whispers, while sweeping that weapon at us,
'Rain-hallowed Graskolnikov, Moosebuggery,
pray let your man go, says this primed arquebus,
or I will kill you all and then make most merry…'

Dear Reader

Murder Bear shaved off all his bloody fur
and sat in the darkness of your kitchen
at the bare careful table you spent so long
scrubbing with salt, rubbing his pate like Kurtz.
The orange oblong of stairlight crayoned
by the doorframe made him grind his teeth.
He filled half the tumbler with Teachers
and topped it up with water. That would learn it.
He spread his papers across your table
and consulted the diagrams that stated
whether you would live or die. Because
he cannot hold the brush, he got you
to make these, although you never knew:
tore the letters from your lists, the glyphs
from your childrens' paintings, the ones
you'd filed away for later or forever,
you weren't sure, but – once he'd aligned them
according to those soft dictators, the moths,
discovered ideograms only the stars
should read, and let your kittens lick his claws –
he knew. You never saw a bear so alone.

Zeichentrickbärendämmerung

1 L'Invitation au Picnic

Only Boo-Boo escaped to tell the tale
of the cartoon bears' big surprise picnic –
the postcard simply claimed, 'THE BLAME
IS YOURS ALONE'. Of course they knew
who it must be from: Murder Bear
has never been in the *Good Bear Guide*.
He punishes the good for when they're bad
and the vice-torn for versa: he is
an equal opportunities ursus; also an
omnidirectional puncher of your sacred snouts;
pincher of the universal vagus; pitcher
of shrieking respectability into the tar pits;
he picks up any wasted rice grains
with other people's still-blinking eyelashes.
Plus the dank vermillion pawprint stank
of Parma violets and horse entrails.
What to do? Well, if there's a murder in Mordor
who you gonna call – Orc-busters?
They kitted up with harpoons, hopelessness
and tasers; they googled for marmalade,
Mamelukes and razors; they goggled up with infra-red,
baked bread and broke out the Brens;
had a brew and filled flasks with liquid nitrogen
to fling in his face of monstrous doubt;
picked out the jams and the gelignite,
said goodnight ladies and sweet princes all
and convoyed by landcruiser for Jellystone…

2 Bonfire of the Teddy Bears

…where each morning Murder Bear would sit
at the feet of Yogi, although these
and his spiritual master's other bits
had to be kept in the deep freeze
overnight. 'What's that, Guru of gore?
Deep in the woods prepare a pickernick
of slaying? Splatter there the average bear?
Get Rupert with a maverick spear?'
Baseball struck by Shoeless never soared so well,
so thunderous a Who-chord never burst
from Marshall stack. Like a crashing satellite
the war-lance (this he claimed to be the digit
of the Cherokee ogress, Spearfinger)
pierced the scarlet jumper's lower hem,
passed unchecked between his trousers' check
and, hissing, sank into the centre of his thigh.
He dumped po' Winnie's body in the well
and his head went bump, bump, bump
down after it, pondering in the last blink
of decapitated thought the distinction
between artesian and arterial, and
do bears eat chairs, or do chairs…
He then did aggro to Hair Bear's afro,
shaving a highway in that wilderness:
a road for the mind control electrodes
which meant, weeping, Aitch took care
of the Bunch himself, rubbed Bubbi up

the wrong way on the tongue-grater,
served Square rare as Forlorne sausage…

3 An Etiology of Murder Bear

Who was not to be spared especially?
Baloo and Beorn to be shown the bare
excessities; Jeremy to go through the ricer
and be puffed, Shardik shredded, and Sooty
to have the insanity claws inserted,
Biffo to drink invisible ink; the Hofmeister,
G, plus Fozzie, B, to sup with horrors, H;
from an island in Baffled Bay would-be
whale-watchers to hear a beluga's strangled cry,
'The Great God Alan Measles is dead!'

Thence to repair to a bar on 39th
between the river delta features of Wystan
and the large crow stabbing a shot glass,
and to bewail 'Gone, all gone; dead for
a duck-caller or possibly a duck-walk –
I got confused toward the end or even
the beginning – now how shall we ever know
the reason why, O rare Mongolian Bear,
or Spirit Bear of British Columbia, or…' (a pause)
'insert a third bear species of your choosing…'

That giant faithless head, that would crush
a shoulder, crashing to the bar; a snore,
that rattled Dylan in St James Infirmary
as though he were a bottle on a shelf;
while across the nation, in a daze,
husbands put down axes, wives
relinquish knives, punks step away from
the pistol; sickles, pitchforks, lose their gleam,
professors pause at chalkboards, poets
put down their glasses and their pens.

Goldilocks comes out of the shower and says
to the dilating eyes of Baby Bear:
'What a strange dream I had, Babes.'
I know, Honey, I know: I was there.

*

Exeunt omnes, pursued by Murder Bear

Cover design and typeset by Liam Relph.
Type set in Arnhem Fine.
Printed by Aldgate Press,
Units 5 & 6,
Gunthorpe Street Workshops,
3 Gunthorpe Street,
London, E1 7RQ.

Number   of 250 copies.

Donut
press
www.donutpress.co.uk